Transportation
Machines
At Work

Trains

By Hal Rogers

SCHOLASTIC INC.

New York   Toronto   London   Auckland   Sydney
Mexico City   New Delhi   Hong Kong   Buenos Aires

Contents

On the Job

On the job, trains carry people and **freight** from place to place. Trains have **locomotives** that pull cars behind them.

Trains have metal wheels that roll

along metal railroad tracks.

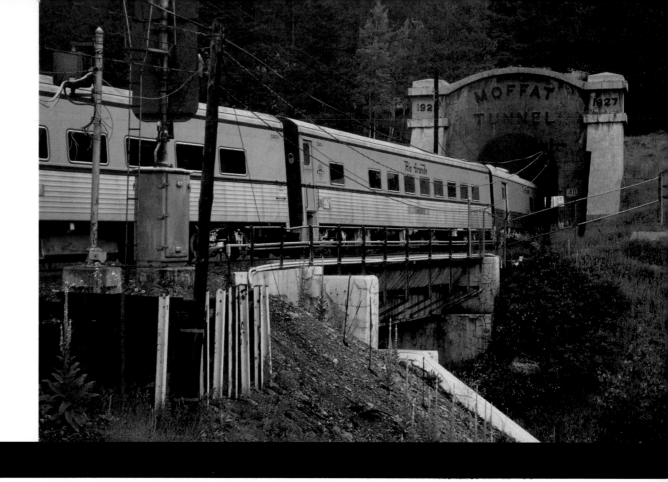

Sometimes trains travel through tunnels. A tunnel is a long hole dug through a hill or mountain.

This freight train carries coal. Other trains carry big things, such as cars and trucks. Trains even carry mail from city to city.

People travel on **passenger** trains. Each
car has a door where the people may
board. Passengers must have tickets to
ride the train. The **conductor** collects
tickets from the passengers.

Another worker takes care of the passengers' suitcases. He puts the suitcases in the **baggage car.**

Passenger cars have many seats. On long trips, people eat their meals on the train. They can visit a special dining car to order food.

The conductor helps connect two train cars. Train cars are connected with **couplers.** These strong hooks hold the cars together, no matter how fast the train goes.

Years ago, all trains had a **caboose.** It was the small car at the end of a train where the brakeman rode. Today, few trains have a caboose because the brakes work automatically on modern trains.

The last car on a modern train has a flashing red light. It helps people see the train.

Climb Aboard!

Would you like to see where the driver sits?

The driver of a train is called an **engineer.**

The engineer sits in the **cab.** The cab is inside

the locomotive. There are many **controls** in

the cab. The engineer has a special telephone.

It is called a **radio.** The engineer uses the

radio to talk to the other train workers.

Up Close

The inside

1. The radio

2. The controls

3. The engineer's seat

The outside

1. The tracks

2. The cab

3. The locomotive

4. The wheels

5. The passenger cars

6. The freight cars

Glossary

baggage car (BAG-edj KAR)
A baggage car is a special car on a train where suitcases and other large items are stored.

board (BORD)
When people board a train, they get on it. Passenger cars have doors where people may board.

cab (KAB)
A cab is where a train's engineer sits. The cab has many controls and a seat for the engineer.

caboose (kuh-BOOSS)
A caboose is a small car at the end of a train. Years ago, train workers rode in cabooses.

conductor (kun-DUK-tur)
A conductor is the worker in charge of the train. The conductor helps connect train cars and collects passengers' tickets.

controls (kun-TROLZ)
Controls are buttons, switches, and other tools that make a machine work. The engineer uses controls to run the train.

couplers (CUP-lerz)
Couplers are giant hooks used to connect train cars. The conductor helps connect the couplers.

engineer (en-jin-EER)
An engineer is a person who drives a train. The engineer sits in the cab.

freight (FRAYT)
Freight is something that a train carries. A freight train can carry coal, mail, or other things.

locomotives (loh-koh-MOH-tivz)
Locomotives are giant engines that move trains. Locomotives pull or push other railroad cars along the tracks.

passenger (PASS-en-jer)
A passenger is a traveler in a vehicle such as a bus, car, train, or airplane. Many people ride on passenger trains.

radio (RAY-dee-o)
A radio lets people talk back and forth without wires. The engineer uses a radio to talk to workers in another train car or at the station.